THE DUKERIES

by

Jessica Garner

BRADWELL
BOOKS

Veteran tree Sherwood Forest – Mark Titterton

Published by Bradwell Books
9 Orgreave Close Sheffield S13 9NP
Email: books@bradwellbooks.co.uk

1st Edition
ISBN – 9781910551646

Text by – Jessica Garner

Typeset by – Mark Titterton

Print – Gomer Press, Llandysul, Ceredigion SA44 4JL

Photograph Credits – Sally Outram, Creswell Heritage Trust,
Creative Commons and others credited individually

Front Cover – Robin Hood / Clumber Park (composite) - Erik Siewko

Back Cover – (top) Clumber Park - Erik Siewko
(middle) Sherwood through the ages - Mark Titterton
(bottom) Creswell Crags - © March 2016 Creswell Heritage Trust

CONTENTS

INTRODUCTION

In the north-west of Nottinghamshire, within an hour of Nottingham city centre, lies the area known as the Dukeries. This name has been used since the 18th century to describe an area that once contained four ducal seats. Beginning around twenty miles north of Nottingham and extending ten miles towards Worksop, the Dukeries is a blend of beautiful old country houses, parkland and forest that is unmatched anywhere else in England.

At most points in England's history, there has been fewer than one ducal family for every two counties. This part of the country is remarkable for having had four in close proximity, and for the fact that the parks belonging to the houses often shared common borders. The sprawling Clumber Park, today run by the National Trust, was owned by the Dukes of Newcastle. Thoresby Hall was the principal seat of the Dukes of Kingston and the Earls Manvers. Welbeck Abbey was founded as a monastery in 1153, and was home to the Dukes of Portland. Worksop Manor, perhaps the grandest of the Dukeries residences in its time, was a seat of the Dukes of Norfolk.

ABOVE: Lime Tree Avenue – Erik Siewko

The four great houses are found around the north of Sherwood Forest, which was once three times its current size. What remains of the ancient woodland is today a national park to be enjoyed by all, where the legend of Robin Hood is still going strong. Other notable sites are Rufford Abbey, once the seat of Lord Savile, and Hodsock Priory, home to various great families over the centuries and renowned for its snowdrops and bluebells. And on the edge of Welbeck Estate, the caves of Creswell Crags contain a world-famous collection of Ice Age artefacts. Each site has a unique history, which we invite you to explore through this guide.

Today, the Dukeries are a thriving visitor destination with something for everyone to enjoy. Discover the history of stately mansions and abbeys, explore the surrounding estates on foot or by bicycle, try your hand at jousting at the Robin Hood Festival, or enjoy traditional afternoon tea in one of many fabulous countryside cafes.

TOP: Thoresby Hall – Sally Outram
BOTTOM: Robin hood statue – Sally Outram

SHERWOOD FOREST

Sherwood Forest once stretched for thirty miles between Nottingham and Worksop, and was part of a royal hunting forest during the 10th century. Areas of the forest were later acquired by nobility, and the four main ducal seats of Clumber, Welbeck, Thoresby and Worksop were established. The last remaining area of ancient woodland is now Sherwood Forest National Nature Reserve. Here, you will find some of the oldest trees in Europe, many of them over five centuries old.

Sherwood is best known as the home of Robin Hood, the mischievous outlaw who robbed the rich to feed the poor with his band of Merry Men. A skilled archer and swordsman, Robin was the bane of sheriffs, barons and prelates, and a much-loved folk figure from medieval times up to the present day.

But there have always been those who are hesitant to dismiss him as purely fictional. The identity of Robin Hood has been debated for centuries, and is one of the last true remaining mysteries of England. One possible candidate is Robert Hod, a tenant of the Archbishop of York and an outlaw in the time of Henry III. Hod was summoned to appear before York Assizes in 1225 and 1226, but fled. In the 17th and 18th centuries, interest in the figure of Robin Hood grew, and he was the subject of several popular plays and poems. 'A True Tale of Robin Hood', a ballad by Martin Parker published in 1632, claimed the real Robin Hood to be the Earl of Huntington. However, the

ABOVE: Robin Hood and Little John's first meeting – creative commons

Veteran oak tree Sherwood Forest – Mark Titterton

antiquarian Roger Dodsworth insisted that it was in fact Robin's companion, Little John, who was the Earl, and that Robin Hood was Robert Loxley, born in South Yorkshire and outlawed for killing his stepfather while ploughing. In 1852, Victorian scholar Joseph Hunter suggested that Robin Hood was one Robert Hood of Wakefield, a supporter of the rebel Earl of Lancaster. After the Earl's defeat at the Battle of Boroughbridge in 1322, the story goes, Robert was pardoned and employed by King Edward, and thereafter known as Robyn Hode. However, it was never proven that the two names really referred to the same man.

The quest to unmask the hooded hero is complicated by the fact that 'Robert' was a common Christian name in medieval England, and was often shortened to 'Robin' or 'Robyn'. The surname 'Hood', sometimes spelled 'Hod' or 'Hode', was also common, referring either to a hooder – a maker of hoods – or to one who sported a hood. As a result, records of people named 'Robin Hood' are many, and often seem to refer to outlaws. The earliest written record of the legend as we know it is the 1377 poem *The Vision of Piers Plowman* by William Langland, which mentions a priest who can recite '*rymes of Robyn Hood*'. However, court records show at least eight people

ABOVE: Sherwood Forest trees – iStock

known as 'Robinhood' before 1300, suggesting that the name may have been an alias used by various thieves, rather than by one particular man.

People's hero, common thief, or pure myth: whoever he was, people have been telling tales of Robin Hood's adventures for over 700 years, and our fascination with him looks set to endure. Each August, around 75,000 visitors flock to the Robin Hood Festival to celebrate the life and times of the world's most famous outlaw with a week of jousting, jesters, and theatre.

The history of Sherwood Forest and its link with Robin Hood is told through the Robyn Hode's Sherwode exhibition at the Sherwood Forest Visitor Centre. The Centre is a ten-minute walk from the village of Edwinstowe, where Robin Hood is said to have married his sweetheart, Maid Marian, in the Church of St Mary. A few hundred yards from the church stands the Major Oak, a colossal tree whose hollow trunk is known as the famous outlaw's hideout. Having stood at the heart of the forest for around 800 years, the great oak still produces acorns to this day.

Robin Hood Festival performers – Sally Outram

Sherwood Forest National Nature Reserve covers 450 acres of ancient woodland, and is remarkable for its variety of wildlife and birdlife. Follow in the footsteps of Robin Hood along the Robin Hood Way long-distance footpath, using either a guidebook or an audio guide to the highlights of the route. The 105-mile circuit begins at Nottingham Castle, leading across woodland and through vibrant market towns, taking in King John's Palace and Newark Castle, and ending at the church in Edwinstowe.

The entire route would take a seasoned walker a week to complete, though there are plenty of circular routes than can be taken as day walks. A free leaflet available from the Visitor Centre allows visitors to guide themselves around the Blue Trail, a 45-minute path circling the Major Oak. The Green Trail  along the Longhorn Cattle enclosure takes around an hour, while the Red Trail is two hours long and leads around the forest.

CRESWELL CRAGS

Creswell Crags is a spectacular limestone gorge that lies on the border between Derbyshire and Nottinghamshire, and is part of the greater Creswell Heritage Landscape Area. These remarkable caves have yielded evidence of life in the last Ice Age, making the site of national importance and a fascinating day out.

Remains excavated from the caves date from between 10,000 to 50,000 years ago, and show that hyena, mammoth and woolly rhinoceros once roamed here. Stone and bone tools have also been discovered, suggesting that the caves provided shelter for nomadic hunter tribes as they tracked migrating prey. The caves are home to the northernmost examples of cave art in Europe, and the only known Ice Age cave art in Britain. Owing to its unique features, Creswell has been designated a Site of Special Scientific Interest.

TOP: Creswell Crags – Visitor Entrance – © March 2016 Creswell Heritage Trust
BOTTOM: Robin Hood Cave at Creswell Crags – © March 2016 Creswell Heritage Trust

Creswell Crags landscape – © March 2016 Creswell Heritage Trust

The site is open to the public daily from February to October, and on weekends for the rest of the year. Tours of the caves run on weekends, offering visitors the chance to learn more about this remarkable site. Delve deeper into the history of Creswell Crags on an Ice Age tour through the Robin Hood Cave, the largest on the site, or take the Rock Art tour around Church Hole Cave to see beautiful engravings of animals and birds that are around 13,000 years old.

Lake at Creswell Crags – © March 2016 Creswell Heritage Trust

To the east end of the gorge is the Museum and Education Centre, displaying some of the rarest objects from the caves, including a rather imposing stuffed hyena. As well as the permanent Ice Age exhibition, the Museum hosts temporary exhibitions in partnership with the Natural History Museum and provides regular talks and activities. Visitors are free to wander around the lake and gorge, and enjoy refreshments from the coffee shop on an open terrace overlooking the magnificent landscape. Those wishing to venture further can take the Crags Loop walk, a seven-mile trail starting at the Centre and leading around the nearby limestone gorge of Markland and Hollinhill Grips. Fossils, cards and books from the shop make lovely gifts or souvenirs.

CLUMBER PARK

Clumber Park in Worksop covers over 3,800 acres of picturesque parkland, heath and woods run by the National Trust. The land was part of Sherwood Forest until 1707, when the Duke of Newcastle enclosed it as a hunting park for Queen Anne. Today, it is open to visitors all year round.

Chapel at Clumber Park – Sally Outram

Clumber grounds – Sally Outram

Heidrun Humphries

The Clumber spaniel was bred at Clumber Park in Nottinghamshire, family home of the Duke of Newcastle. The breed supposedly came from France to Britain at the time of the French Revolution, when the Duke received a kennel of the dogs from the Duc de Noailles. Coloured white with lemon or orange markings, the Clumber is said to be of an affable nature.

The breed's history is uncertain before the mid-19th century. One story goes that the now extinct Alpine Spaniel was bred with Basset Hounds and the Pyrenean Mountain Dog to produce the Clumber; another says they descended from the Blenheim Spaniel. During World War I, breeding stopped completely and their numbers decreased to a record low until 1925, when King George V redeveloped them in the Royal Kennel. Once large gundogs, the modern breed is smaller although still used as a gundog as well as family pet.

Prince Albert, the Prince consort of Queen Victoria, was a Clumber fancier and promoter, as was his son King Edward VII, who bred them at the Sandringham estate in Norfolk. An entry in Queen Victoria's diary on October 16, 1840, reads: "Walked out directly after breakfast before Albert went to shoot. He had his seven fine Clumber Spaniels with us … They are such dear, nice dogs."

The prestigious Best in Show prize was won by a Clumber spaniel, Sh. Ch. Raycroft Socialite, at the 1991 Crufts Centenary Show. The breed is recognised as a Vulnerable Native Breed, with fewer than 300 new registrations annually.

Clumber was the country estate of the Dukes of Newcastle for three centuries. The approach to Clumber is the three-mile Duke's Drive, or Lime Tree Avenue, the longest avenue of lime trees in Europe and magnificent to behold on foot, by bicycle or by car. Though the mansion was demolished in 1939, hints of its grand past survive. A stable yard and ornate entrance lodges are still standing, along with beautiful 19th century glasshouses featuring a working apiary.

Venture along an avenue of cedar trees to the pleasure grounds, designed by the 2nd Duke in the late 18th century for picnicking, walking and boating. All these activities can still be enjoyed here today. A little further on, you will find the four-acre Walled Kitchen Garden, one of the park's most fabulous sights. Wander the pathways among hundreds of varieties of fruits and vegetables, a rose garden and cut flower borders.

Bicycles can be hired from the visitor centre and are a wonderful way to explore the park. Walking maps and routes are available from the shop to guide you through the woods and heathland on foot, taking in the vibrant wildlife as you go. At the heart of the estate, a serpentine lake provides ample opportunity for fishing and

ABOVE: Glasshouses and kitchen garden at Clumber – Sally Outram

birdwatching. The view from the classical bridge here is renowned as one of the most beautiful in England, where you can still see the *'proud-chested swans which sail gently in numbers to and fro'*, as described by the historian John Throsby on his visit in 1796.

Younger visitors can learn more about Clumber's wildlife at the Discovery Centre with activities and talks. The Clumber café offers a splendid menu based around fresh seasonal produce from the Walled Kitchen Garden. Visit the gift shop for a beautiful range of locally made souvenirs. There is also a well-stocked plant shop and second-hand book shop.

RUFFORD ABBEY

Rufford Abbey, found two miles south of Ollerton, is a 12th-century former Cistercian monastery and the best-preserved remains of its kind in England. After the Reformation, Rufford became a country house and served as the seat of the Savile family, or Earls of Scarborough. In 1952, the grand abbey and 150 acres of its

ABOVE: Clumber Lake – Sally Outram

grounds were purchased by Nottinghamshire County Council and transformed into Rufford Abbey Country Park. The estate is open all year round, and admission is free.

An ever-popular tourist attraction, Rufford has been voted the top place to visit in Nottinghamshire. There's plenty to see and do in the grounds, including the Wheel of Fortune maze, children's play village, and giant lawn chess. The formal gardens are a peaceful place to sit, play croquet or enjoy stunning displays of blooms, shrubs and herbs. A sculpture trail, the only public sculpture park in Nottinghamshire, is a must-see, featuring 25 unique works collected by Rufford over the last three decades.

ABOVE: Rufford Abbey – Sally Outram

A firm favourite with visitors is a leisurely twenty-minute walk around the lake. Other routes of between eight and fourteen miles explore the surrounding areas of Sherwood Heath, Old Ollerton and Wellow, with stunning views and  plenty of tea rooms and pubs along the way. The lawns to one side of the Abbey make the perfect spot for picnics and games.

TOP: Rufford Abbey garden path – Sally Outram
ABOVE: Looking across the park – Sally Outram

At Rufford Craft Centre, housed in the former stable block, visitors can get involved in creative workshops with professional artists and view exhibitions on the life of Rufford's medieval monks. A detailed guide to the history of Rufford is available from the book and gift shop. Meals and afternoons teas are served in the superb Savile Restaurant, set in the original kitchen of the old country residence, while the Coach House Café and the Mill Teashop offer a welcome snack or hot drink after a walk.

Several times a year, the Abbey dedicates its grounds to special events, from the Earth and Fire International Ceramics Festival in June to the renowned Aurora Winter Illuminations in December, when the gardens are lit up after dark in spectacular colours.

THORESBY HALL

Thoresby Hall in Ollerton is a majestic Grade I listed building, once home to the Earls and Dukes of Kingston. The original house was destroyed by fire in 1746. The 2nd Duke's nephew, Charles Meadows, inherited Thoresby in 1786 as the first Earl Manvers. He oversaw several improvements to the house, and Sydney Pierrepont, the 3rd Earl Manvers, commissioned renowned architect Anthony Salvin to build the new hall at Thoresby in 1864. Today the building

TOP: Rufford Abbey interior – James Hill
BOTTOM: Rufford Abbey – James Hill

has been fully restored by Warner Holidays, right down to the silk damask on the walls, as one of their Historic Hotels. The Pierrepont family still take an active part in the site's management.

Thoresby's romantic countryside setting has made it a popular venue for weddings. Guests on day visits, weekend breaks or longer stays can enjoy a variety of activities. A luxurious spa offers massage, a sauna and relaxation treatments from

TOP: Thoresby Hall – Sally Outram
BOTTOM: Thoresby Hall Courtyard – Sally Outram

around the world, followed by a two-course lunch or champagne afternoon tea. There are also plenty of opportunities to get active with archery, fencing, yoga and dance classes.

Day visitors are welcome to look around the Hall's magnificent interiors and stroll in the grounds. On open days in the Victorian rose garden, you will find the Thoresby Hall Rose, a fragrant and deep crimson flower unique to Thoresby. The surrounding Thoresby Park is perfect for picnics, and has signposted walks that meander around thousands of acres of forest and farmland. A variety of fairs and shows take place on the lawns throughout the year, including music, theatre and the Notts Classic Car and Motorcycle Show, held at Thoresby for nearly a quarter of a century.

Thoresby Gallery was established in 1992 to house the Pierrepont Collection. The gallery now runs a lively programme of exhibitions with a special focus on local artists, and is open every day except Monday. The thriving Thoresby Courtyard holds many a delight, from shops selling beautifully crafted jewellery and homewares, fine wines and children's toys, to a glass-blowing studio and craft workshops. Relax over lunch at the Bay Tree Café, and take home delicious local produce from the Sherwood Game and Farm shop.

WORKSOP MANOR

Worksop Manor is an 18th-century country house, seat of the ancient Lords of Worksop. The site is closed to the public today, though there are walks around Clumber, Welbeck and Hardwick that give excellent views of the house. From  the 14th century, the Manor was owned by the Talbot family, the Earls of Shrewsbury. Mary, Queen of Scots was imprisoned there

ABOVE: Worksop Manor in the mid-18th century – Creative Commons

during 1568, and King James I famously stayed at the house in 1603 on his way south to take the English throne. At the end of the 17th century, it passed to the Duke of Norfolk, and remained in his family until 1840, when it was sold to the Duke of Newcastle of nearby Clumber Park. Traditionally, the Lord of the Manor of Worksop would assist at the coronation of the British monarch by providing a white glove, a practice that continued into the 1950s.

The market town of Worksop is known as the 'Gateway to the Dukeries', and makes an excellent place to start a tour of the area. The paving on Bridge Street bears the crests of the great families who owned the nearby houses of Rufford, Thoresby, Clumber and Welbeck, set in coloured stone. A special attraction is Mr Straw's House, home to a grocer and his family during the 1920s. The humble semi-detached Edwardian house is today a miniature museum, containing furnishings and possessions laid out just as the Straws left them. Walter Straw's cacti collection can be seen still thriving in the greenhouse outside.

ABOVE: Path to Worksop Priory Gatehouse – Sally Outram

The magnificent Worksop Priory is one of the area's best-known landmarks, founded as an Augustinian priory in 1103. Though most of the building was demolished at the Dissolution, the main priory church remained, and continues to be used as the parish church. The priory's gatehouse has served many purposes over the centuries. It was an elementary school in 1628, a 'school for poor boys' around 1853, and most recently provided shelter for the homeless, a service of which its pious founders would surely be proud. The Gatehouse exterior, featuring statues of St Augustine, St Cuthbert and the Holy Trinity, is truly a sight to behold.

Worksop Priory Gatehouse – Sally Outram

HODSOCK PRIORY

The historic country house of Hodsock Priory is set in the 800-acre Hodsock Estate, four miles north of Worksop. Despite its name, the house has never in fact been a priory. From the 12th century to the present day, Hodsock has been home to the Cressey, Clifton and Mellish families, before passing in 1966 to Sir Andrew Buchanan, 5th Baronet, whose descendants still occupy it today. George Buchanan, his wife Katherine and their four children live in the old servants' quarters, while the rest of the house has been restored to serve as a popular venue for weddings and other events.

ABOVE: Hodsock snowdrops – Courtesy Hodsock Priory

TOP: Hodsock Priory – Courtesy Hodsock Priory
BOTTOM: Hodsock Priory Gatehouse – Courtesy Hodsock Priory

Though the house is generally closed to the public, tours run on weekdays for groups of 20 to 50. Visitors can discover the rich heritage of Hodsock through history talks, browse the Hodsock archives, and enjoy an afternoon tea, two-course lunch, or simply a hot drink and snack as part of their tour. For smaller groups and individuals, Secrets of Hodsock evenings take place a few times a year.

Hodsock is best known for its stunning displays of flowers. Around February, the five acres of formal gardens surrounding the house come alive with fabulous winter blooms such as hellebores, irises and winter honeysuckle. However, the real jewel in Hodsock's crown is the flurry of snowdrops that appear in the spring. During February and early March, the famed Snowdrop Gardens welcome visitors to stroll among the delicate white flowers, which cover around five acres of the estate.

There are walks to suit everyone, with shortcuts for those less mobile and longer routes for visitors keen to explore the surrounding woodland. George Buchanan is normally on hand every day from 2pm to give talks about Hodsock's past and the history of its flowers. Bulbs and potted snowdrops are available from the plant sale as the perfect souvenir of Hodsock.

Later in the spring, the Horsepasture Wood is transformed into the Bluebell Wood by a carpet of fragrant blue flowers. A sight not to be missed, the wood is open to the public for two weekends in early May.

WELBECK ABBEY

Welbeck Abbey lies within Welbeck Estate, an area of great natural beauty covering 15,000 acres between Sherwood Forest and Clumber Park. The abbey was founded as a monastery in 1153, and following the Dissolution was acquired by Charles Cavendish, son of Bess of Hardwick, in 1607. It then passed to his son, William John Cavendish, 1st Duke of Newcastle. Perhaps Welbeck's most eccentric owner, William lived in a small series of rooms within the vast abbey, and employed hundreds of workmen to carve out an underground maze including a library, a ballroom, and a network of tunnels wide enough for a horse and carriage. In the 18th century, Welbeck passed to the Bentinck family and became the seat of the Earls and Dukes of Portland.

Though today the Abbey is a private family home, visitors can wander the old walled gardens, and tours of the grand State Rooms run for 28 days in August. Visitors can view pieces from the historic

Welbeck Abbey.

View of Welbeck Abbey, 1910 – Courtesy of www.picturethepast.org.uk

TOP AND BOTTOM: Welbeck Courtyard – Sally Outram

Portland Collection, one of the largest privately owned collections of British portraits. Stair-free tours are also available, allowing more time to explore the ground-floor rooms.

Welbeck Estate is a thriving community and home to several unique businesses. One of its newer ventures is the Welbeck Abbey Brewery, housed in a listed barn and producing quality cask ales and bottled beers. Guided tours allow visitors an insight into the brewing process from start to finish, perfectly rounded off with a pint of

ABOVE: Welbeck Abbey gates – Sally Outram

Welbeck ale. The Welbeck Farm Shop has earned a reputation as one of the best in the country, selling produce from Nottinghamshire and neighbouring counties and from the Estate itself. Take home some Welbeck Bakehouse bread, ales from the brewery, or a block of Stichelton, a raw milk blue cheese made exclusively at Welbeck.

The Harley Gallery has an exciting programme of exhibitions, events and workshops running all year round. Visit the craft shop, see displays by local artists and enjoy a homemade meal at the Harley Café, a favourite among locals. A circular walk beginning at the Gallery takes visitors through the estate's stunning scenery and on to Creswell Crags and the Holbeck.